Keep growing
+ Keep GOING!

PIVOTING WITH PURPOSE

THE HAMSTER WHEEL, THE RAT RACE, AND OTHER CAREER MYTHS HOLDING YOU BACK

BY MELISA MERAL

Cover design & photos by Wakebone Creative
Edited by Stefanie Histed
Printed in the United States of America

[FOR THOSE WHO ARE READY
TO MAKE SHT HAPPEN]

Table of Contents

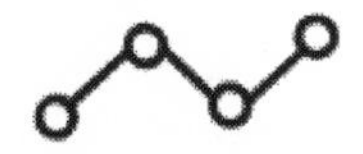

PREFACE

So, you followed the rules of "go to college, get a job, and buy a home with a white picket fence." Are you happy now? Or are you feeling stuck and not sure how to get out of living paycheck to paycheck, clocking in and clocking out, and drowning in your sense of being unfulfilled?

This hasn't turned out to be your "dream life" has it? You have bills to pay (and maybe kids to feed) so you surely need an income. But, what if there was a better-aligned role for YOU and your natural skills, talents, and abilities?

"Oh, but the job market is too competitive, and I am just so lucky to have a life that's good enough."

Really? Don't you want more out of life?

You have probably been told your entire time on this earth that work is work, a job is a job, a paycheck is a paycheck, and it's not going to be a peachy-keen, roses-and-rainbows-filled life. These myths were most likely modeled by your parents and societal norms. And here you are, stuck thinking you have to work a job you hate just to make enough money to survive.

Secretly, you want to like (or even LOVE) what you are doing Monday-Friday 6 am to 6 pm. But how can you get there? It starts with the inner work of diving into your own limiting beliefs and changing your mindset to opt into that life of abundance so that you can stop living in fear. It's time to tap into your own inner greatness and let those gifts that you already have within you, SHINE.

I'm talkin' resume at the top of the pile, zero competition because you're role-aligned and value-aligned in your job search, and not an ounce of fear of rejection because you know you are on the right path no matter what comes your way. Doesn't that sound a lot better than where you are now?

Stop settling for a life that is just "good enough." Get ready to explore your personal values, emotional intelligence, and strengths. You can gain special job search superpowers by simply tapping into those childhood dreams that are dying in your heart. Start checking things off your bucket list and let's find the best job, position, company, and team that will set you off on your next big life journey. Buckle up as you attempt to unlock your mindset and release those anchors holding you down. Break free from the chains holding you back and land the job of your dreams!

"Live in abundance and wealth, not fear."

- a random massage therapist providing advice from the table in 2011

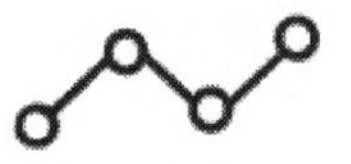

INTRODUCTION

It was a dreary Monday morning. I spent the whole evening before, feeling the "Sunday Scaries." You know those moments — that bittersweet feeling that the weekend is ending, and the workweek is looming. I arrived early at my cubicle before my boss (Human Resources' version of Miranda Priestly in the Devil Wears Prada) arrived to make my life a living hell. Cutthroat. A beast in business. But also, a total b*tch. I consider myself thick-skinned and not one to easily back down from a confrontation but working with this woman was a whole new ball game. She had this passive-aggressive way of belittling everyone she came into contact with, except of course those above her in role and position. The ultimate oozing of insecurity — in the most impolite way. I was making six figures — as a 28-year-old — and every bone in my body hated it. Over those years I truly learned what "money doesn't buy you happiness" means.

So, what did I do about it? Well, after miscarrying the child I was bearing with my fiancé, I decided to call it quits. But not just a mental health break on disability. Or a resignation notice with plenty of time to find a new role. No — I did it the Melisa way and resigned the very next day. Because if you're going to go out, go out with a bang.

"Leap, and the net will appear."
-John Burroughs

Or so I thought. I had a side hustle running in the background (which I think everyone should have — and we'll get into that later) but it was making no way near my six-fig salary. On my first day of being "funemployed," I quickly watched hundreds of YouTube videos on how to grow a business, subscribed to every entrepreneur podcast I could get my ears on, and filled out freebie worksheet after freebie worksheet in an attempt to get my proverbial sht together.

By January 1st 2018, I had a real, live, Limited Liability Company (more commonly referred to as an "LLC"). I called it Make SHT Happen and ordered a Doing Business As (DBA) along with the name of Let's Get You

Organized, which is what my side hustle had been named as I was paid "under the table."

Follow your dream, they said. Listen to your heart, they said. Feel the fear and do it anyway, they said. It will be fun, they said. Two years later and a significant amount of money gone (*cough* my entire life savings) ... I decided it was time to get a job, you know before I incurred some like *serious* debt.

Being a small business owner was hard. But looking for a job after being out of the game for two years was harder.

How do you explain that your boss was a twat, so you left in a fiery fury of rage and launched a company with a swear word in the name, only to lose all your money and end up back where you started? Well, first off, you don't. You ever-so-delicately explain that two-year gap on your resume and try to overemphasize why you'll make a great employee even though you've had a taste of being your own boss. "Yes! I love taking direction!" "Oh, I'm totally good with being managed." "For sure, I have a servant leadership mindset so I'm always here to help YOU." And all that bullshit.

So that's what this book is about. It's for the burnt-out entrepreneurs that need the stability and security of a paycheck again. It's for the normal people that had to take a few years off because life or kids or death happened. It's how to re-enter an ever-changing workforce.

Toto, we most definitely aren't in Kansas anymore.

The world of work is a brand-new frontier post-COVID and we're here for it. Telecommuting (aka working from home in your PJs more likely with a messy bun and coffee stains than on a beach somewhere tropical living the #laptoplife — let's keep it real), your boss focused more on company culture and employee engagement than shiny suits and fancy titles, and a digital culture that honors results, commitment, and loyalty.

Let's cut the crap when it comes to looking for a job and get down to the real talk.

Twat boss lady changed my life. Those sayings “it was a blessing in disguise” and “hindsight is 20/20” totally made sense in this case. Webster’s dictionary definition of “catalyst” is a person or thing that precipitates an event. That cataclysmic event was quitting my job, starting a business, “finding myself,” and then re-entering the workforce as a better human being because of it. Thanks, twat boss. You’re a real pal.

cat·a·lyst
/ˈkad(ə)ləst/
noun

1. **a person or thing that precipitates an event.**

Because here’s the thing ... life happens. At one point or another, we all go through some sht. And the hope is that we become stronger, more resilient, and diamond-like because of those hardships. If you’re looking at your resume going “How the eff am I going to get a job in this city with all this competition in my field?” or “How can I explain this job gap and still make myself sound like the best candidate?” or “WTF do

I even actually want to do? I've hated my past few jobs!" ... then keep reading.

See, we're all products of trauma. We've all gone through the wringer in one way or another. Childhood leaves us with battle wounds. Relationships leave us with broken hearts. Failure leaves us with regret. And on, and on, and on ... and on.

Consider this your golden Willy Wonka ticket to get. the. eff. over. it.

We all remember those cheesy posters in 7th-grade science class full of sea turtles and kittens with words like *Persistence* and *Resilience* on them — corny AF but at the end of the day, those messages do hold some weight. If you've ever read any self-help book, then you know that. But that isn't what we're going to explore together in this book. If you're ready to move on from playing the victim and truly own your sht and circumstance (no pomp and circumstance here) then let's go!

Chapter 1:

Your Stories Don't Own You

Stories are more than just what kids read before bed. They are also what our brain makes up 24/7 (yes, even in our sleep). Constantly judging. Constantly criticizing. Constantly singing old 90s boy band songs. And constantly trying to make sense of the realities of the environment we are in at every given moment. So, we write stories. About our family, our friends, our boss, our coworkers, our cashier at the grocery store, the crow cawing at us on our walk, the dog barking at us at the park, the asshole that cut us off in traffic — it's all one big story that our brain has made up for us. Oh, and for those that suffer from insomnia, y'all get extra special bedtime stories that keep your mind racing and your coffee bill growing.

The first step to bucking up and getting over your trauma is to rewrite those stories that are keeping you tied down. Too scared to apply for that job in Digital Marketing because you've never had a formal title and want to 'follow the rules' because your brain said you have to? Apply to fifteen of them with your awesome, personally branded resume. On the fence about reaching out to that old coworker that lurks on your LinkedIn and has your dream job, but you're worried that he'll ignore you, ghost you, or write you off? Send the damn message already, be genuine about your current state in life, and explain exactly why you're reaching out. Chances are, your brain wrote a story that people couldn't *possibly* want to help you. Rewrite that sht *now*.

For about thirty years, I mostly believed the stories my brain told me. That I had a horrible childhood and I was wounded so I was allowed to be an ass to most everyone. That I was an introvert so that meant I didn't have to get close to people or keep jobs longer than a year. That money didn't grow on trees and I had to struggle to survive.

Do you think any of those stories served me? Do you think any of those thinking patterns contributed to my happiness? Hell no.

This is why I started the book here for you — the importance of understanding that you have the power to rewrite your stories whenever you want, wherever you want, is *key*.

Get out that pen and paper (or digital whatever) and start writing down *all* the stories you've been telling yourself. All the "I can'ts" or "I shouldn'ts". All the limiting beliefs that are holding you back. Believe me when I say they aren't getting you ANYWHERE!

If you want to go a step further, you can watch some YouTube videos or enroll in a Udemy course on Neuro-linguistic Programming. Now, before you call me a narcissistic sales snake or cult leader, just know that NLP changed my life for good once I understood the actual chemical activity in the brain that contributes to our successes (and failures) in life! Understanding leads to knowledge and knowledge gives you the power to observe what's going on day-to-day so that you can change your behavior accordingly. Cue the "More You Know" rainbow...

Quieting the doubters.

You know that the human brain writes little stories about anything and everything, but now can we talk about *other* people? Other people write them too. About you. About what you wear, how you talk, where you hang out, what you drive, how you write your emails, how slow you type, the crappy town you're from, what lame music you listen to, what weird shows you watch, and on and on and on and on. Before you go into a hissy fit... newsflash: it's natural and human and you do it too.

Back in the day I filmed a video and wrote an article for a large SaaS company called Keap by Infusionsoft. It was all about how I came from an immigrant family and as a first-generation American I was taught to live the American dream by going to school, getting good grades, graduating college, and getting a good corporate job before settling down to start a family.

Puke. No. Thank You.

Always the black sheep, I took the entrepreneur route instead (or detour... whichever way you want to look at it!). And now I speak on stages and write books and do other cool sht that *lights me up* and doesn't make me feel like I'm rotting away in a cubicle.

Do you think if I stayed stuck in caring about all the millions of stories people had made up about me in their lil old brains that I would have made any of those moves? Nope. I would've stayed stuck in the gray cubicle crying about the twat boss and just wanting to please my parents by playing it safe and staying in the box they had allotted to me.

It's time to quiet the doubters. They're never going to stop thinking those things or stop judging you. But YOU can control your level of attention to it. Ignore, ignore, ignore.

Where could you go if you stopped relying on validation, recognition, and appreciation from others? No expectations of outcomes in life. No attachments. Get deep. Get quiet.

Reflect and allow the answers to come through!

What happens if some of your closest friends turn into doubters too? Clear away the toxic energy of those who don't believe in you, support you, or even mildly trust you and your newfound vision. Sometimes you have to get in that rocket ship for one (or sometimes there's room for a copilot) and skyrocket yourself into your vision, sans girl gang.

Growth can scare people off. If suddenly you start acting differently, talking differently, and moving differently, it will probably come as a shock to your friends. But are you going to let their opinions stop you from achieving your big, scary, purposeful, dream?

The word *surrender* may come to mind here. Surrender to the fact that you're growing in different directions. Let go of the expectations you have of your friends and the expectations that they have of you. At the end of the day, some will support you and some won't, and that is okay!

Want to move across the country to get out of the bubble you've always grown up in? Do it. Want to dye your hair black and start wearing red lipstick? Go for it. Want to start an Instagram account for your secret love of Pokémon? I'm sure there's a niche for that.

I know you've heard it in all those self-help books before, but seriously life's too short to not do the things you want and to try on all the different identities that are available to you within this lifetime. Get out there and do the damn thing. Oh, and rewrite your stories and quiet the doubters while you're at it.

Pivoting with Purpose Tip

Get out your pen and paper. It's time to rewrite the stories that are holding you back. Are you going to go to your grave with dreams in your heart, just because of what Sharon at the front desk thinks? Or Amy at the gym? Or that chick on Instagram who takes crappy selfies? Or your brother's wife who you don't even like? Write your own damn story and stop listening to everyone else.

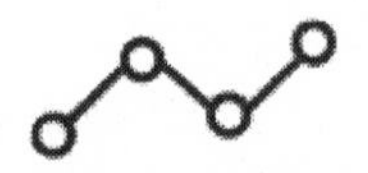

Chapter 2:

What Do You WANT?

"What do you want to be when you grow up?" The most asked question of our childhood, or maybe a close-second behind "Where's the remote?" Every single one of us has natural skills, abilities, talents, and gifts to monetize and share during this lifetime. And no, I'm not going to tell you that you're a pretty little special snowflake.

On stage, I speak about productivity. Do you know how many other keynote speakers are out there speaking on this topic globally? THOUSANDS. I am in no way a unique (or fragile) snowflake. Honestly, we all pretty much talk about the same sht. But I know with every cell in my body that I'm meant to speak, teach, train, motivate and inspire. That's *my* gift and it took me *thirty years* to find it. It's time to find *your* magic. There's room for you, I promise.

When was the last time you asked yourself "What do I want?" And I don't mean a glass of wine, or a flatter tummy, or a Louis Vuitton bag, or a hot boyfriend. Like, what do you WANT? Out of life? Out of legacy? What do you want to leave behind on this earth? Your true timestamp of living? What is it for you?

This is a powerful effing question and one that I hid from for all of my teenage years and most of my young adult life. The magic started happening when I finally dove into it.

Did I WANT to work in HR or was I doing it day after 9 am-5 pm day just because it was a "good job" (said with my dad's heavy Middle Eastern accent)? Did I WANT to work in a gray ass cubicle spouting off phrases like "let's circle back" and "we should chat offline"? Did I WANT to drink five cups of coffee in the morning and five glasses of wine at night just to self-soothe enough to keep me off antidepressants?

HELL NO. I was living a shell of a life because I had never answered that one most powerful question.

Start small. At the moment you are reading this right now, ask yourself a few simple questions. Are you thirsty? Hungry? Tired? Need to use the restroom? Sure, it sounds silly, but quick pulse checks like this throughout the day can become an excellent practice for tapping into what you need and want. Build up bigger with practice to ask yourself if you are committing to calendar obligations that you don't want to attend, calls you don't want to hold, or projects you don't want to say yes to.

Eventually with enough reflection, journaling, meditation, or whatever your thing happens to be (I am not in the hippie-dippy yoga-loving crowd at ALL if you can't tell by now but I love a good journaling sesh with a cup of tea and some ambient music in the background — you do you boo), you'll start to see a few shimmers and glimmers of your vision and purpose.

Without purpose, you can't have hope. I realized this after I spiraled into a deep depression right before I found my dream job. I felt completely purposeless. Like I had failed at my career in Human Resources and like I had failed in my business. Nowhere to go, no one to hire me — wine and Netflix were my only friends. I was NOT turning out to be a healthy job seeker. It was like there was nothing to look forward to, only rejection after rejection. And no pile of self-help books, or free guided meditations, or mantras written in lipstick on my bathroom mirror were going to fix that.

I had to figure out my *purpose*. I always knew that I was meant for more. Meant for something bigger. Like I had only scratched the surface on my life's potential. And if you are anything like me, then I am sure you are feeling that way too.

That's where I go back to the question of "What do you want to be when you grow up?" It can sound so trivial but stick with me here. It could be the reason you wanted to be a veterinarian is simply that you loved animals, or the reason you wanted to be a flight attendant is that you wanted to travel and have adventures, or the reason you wanted to be a doctor is that you wanted to help people (or you were a boss at the game *Operation* and thought you could monetize your talents like the true hustler that you are... either way).

Can we get back to that level of simplicity? Why have we made choosing our passions *so* complicated as adults? Instead, we toil and grind away in jobs we hate with people we hate at companies we hate in cities we hate, all because mediocrity has become the norm. A life that's just "good enough" has become the norm.

Glimmers of a vision.

I was alphabetizing the magazines in my older brother's orthodontist office while he was in headgear appointments when I was five years old.

Alphabetizing. Magazines. What?

That was around the age when I told my mom I wanted to be a "cleaning lady" when I grew up. I launched Let's Get You Organized in 2011 where my specialty was cleaning out, decluttering, and organizing pantries, garages, and closets. Dreams do come true. Even for cleaning ladies.

For several years after that, I also wanted to be a teacher. I was the sassy little girl bossing all of her friends around, standing at the front of the "classroom" (aka my bedroom), and creating little homework packets for them at night, writing "lesson plans" on my easel in our family's garage until my dad made me go to bed. I come from a long line of teachers — my mom was a teacher, my grandma was a teacher, my dad was a college professor, my grandpa's mom was a teacher, and several of my aunts and uncles also work in education.

And now (after about 25 years of running in circles), I am a keynote speaker and interactive workshop leader. See? It's simple. That was my vision. And it always has been!

What is the vision you have for *your* life? When you close your eyes and imagine the one or two things that give you energy, motivate you like no other, and absolutely LIGHT YOU UP? What does your ideal day look like?

It's an easy way out to say "Well, I don't feel that way about anything." Sorry sister, but we are not meant to live mundane, boring, vanilla, bland, "good enough" lives. You are meant for *more*. We both know you're better than that excuse. So, what is it? Cooking? Baking? Gardening? Aerial arts? CrossFit? Surfing? Composting? Coding? Copywriting? Tarot reading? Ceramic pottery art? Crocheting? I could ramble on but it's probably better if you hit up the Googs and search "hobbies", check out an app like Groupon to see which new activities you could try in your area, or poke around Pinterest and whip up some ideas.

Upon first look, it might be a slight, tentative, nod toward "Yea ... I guess that's fine and I kind of like doing that" but I urge you to dig deeper! When you find it, you'll *feel it*.

"But Melisa, what do you mean *feel it*? Like how we're supposed to *feel it* when we meet our soulmate?"

Let me explain.

At my twat boss lady job, I had one tiny glimmering moment of my purpose. I was tasked with helping organize a Leadership Retreat for all of our C-Level Executives and Directors with cross-functional teams throughout our giant Fortune 500 company. The first day of the retreat came and the MC (did you know that meant Master of Ceremonies? Because I didn't know that until I was 28 years old.) didn't show up.

I stepped up to the plate, grabbed the mic, and legitimately had a Harry-Potter-holding-his-wand-for-the-first-time moment.

The world made sense with a microphone in my hand. The words coming out of my mouth in my signature, high-energy way. No shaking, no faltering. All out confidence and excitement that I got to have all eyes on me. Call me selfish, call me a brag, call me an attention whore, but you know what? For the very first time in my entire adult life, I felt *true joy* that day. And even though it took me several years to feel that again on stage (because as you know, sometimes we forget and life happens), that was the first step.

"The meaning of life is to find your gift. The purpose of life is to give it away."

-debatably by Pablo Picasso but no one really knows, believe me, I Googled it, and everything

I want you to find your gift. I want you to share your gift. And it can totally become a side hustle if it is not something you can monetize full time yet! But if it is anything like my big vision, there are *plenty* of jobs where I could make a big fat paycheck utilizing my greatest gifts and talents. If sht hit the fan, I could apply for hundreds, if not *thousands* of Corporate Trainer, Executive Coach, Leadership Development Manager, Professor, or Teacher's Assistant roles across the globe. Figure out what you want to do and do it.

Pivoting with Purpose Tip

Groundhog Day doesn't have to be your life. Ask yourself the one most powerful question and let everything else fall into place.

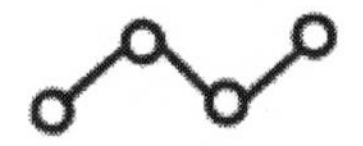

Chapter 3:

Find Your Zone of Greatness

I have dual citizenship in the US and Turkey. One entire side of my family lives in Turkey, and they've never even been to America! Our home is in a rural area of the country — I'm talkin' people without running water or electricity, living on farms with nothing but chickens and goats to keep them company.

On one recent trip, I remember driving past a group of women on the side of the road, thinking to myself "Where do they find their sense of *purpose*?" Without purpose, what are we? Without purpose, where is the hope, the motivation, the excitement, the *lust for life* that Iggy Pop so eloquently told us about?

Three years ago, I was a burnt-out corporate rat racer that desired one thing: freedom. On my journey to figure out what freedom meant for me, I realized I did not have to stay in that crazy world of climbing the corporate ladder. I started thinking about how I could leave my six-figure position at a Fortune 500 company. I discovered that I could monetize my passion, which at the time was decluttering the homes of San Diego residents (aka professional home organizing) you know, like Marie Kondo, but the sassier, feistier version.

My thoughts started swirling after that thought popped into my head. Will I make money? Is this a good idea? What will my dad think? By the way, he has a Ph.D. in molecular biophysics, my mom has a master's degree, and no one in the family is an entrepreneur. Those thoughts quickly turned into actual physical feelings of *fear*. My ego was yelling at me: "This does not feel safe! This does not seem like a logical decision to leave a corporate six-figure job in a career you have worked so hard to build! No one in your family is an entrepreneur! What makes you think you can do this?!"

Have you ever felt those nagging feelings of fear? Have you ever run into any doubters along your journey? You know, the haters and the trolls. We all have. And I am going to let you in on a little secret — they never go away!

You might be wondering how I went from that scared and miserable career btch with the corner office to where I am now. What was the turning point for me? It was the moment I decided to *fight.* I left the corporate world. I felt the fear and I did it anyway. I stopped caring what my family and friends thought of me leaving *their* version of a "dream job" and dove right into full-time entrepreneurship. I quieted the doubters and kicked my ego to the curb.

With my dreams of being a schoolteacher long gone since those late nights in my childhood, I'd almost completely forgotten about my love for speaking on stage. It hit me like a wave crashing over my entire body the second I picked up that mic at my Leadership Retreat. I wanted to cry. I wanted to shriek. I wanted to shout it from the rooftops. I, Melisa Meral, *had found my purpose*.

After that magical moment, I went to several motivational business conferences where speaker after speaker *wowed* me. From then on, I knew with every cell in my body that this is what I'm meant to do with my life. This is my *gift*. This is my *purpose*.

On the journey of finding your inherently natural and awesome gifts and talents, ask yourself "Am I still focusing on the sht I'm not good at?" American culture has this amazing obsession with focusing on weaknesses instead of strengths. Advertisements constantly bombard us with messages like "Get rid of your belly fat once and for all!" or "Learn how to invest in real estate without any prior knowledge!" or "Enroll today to get your next credential so you can land your dream job!" All implying that we need to get better, that we need to fix ourselves, that we need to improve, and that we're inherently not ever going to be *enough*.

In summary: it's a bunch of noise that keeps us from doubling down on our strengths and staying in our lane while we are at it.

Go deep instead of wide. The deeper you go into your purpose, the closer you are to finding your absolute zone of greatness. The zone where you are most productive, most energized, and most motivated by the work you do every single day. It is where doing the sht you truly LOVE to do meets the sht you can get PAID to do, while also impacting others and changing the world for the better.

Like a Venn diagram full of fireworks and sparks of chemistry. Doesn't that just sound absolutely juicy? Instead of focusing on changing the crap about yourself (that past the age of 25 your brain is probably not planning on changing anyway), let's focus on emphasizing what we are *really fkn good at* already.

Listen to the whispers. Chances are, you have already been told by multiple people throughout your life that you have certain strengths and gifts. I bet you are already starting to use and share them! Look closely.

Am I great at being diplomatic, tactful, poised, soft, gentle, or patient? Nope. That's why when I set out to find my next best job, company, and team, I didn't search at all in finance, engineering, politics, behavioral health (social work, therapy, psychiatry), Human Resources (again), or anything else that would cause me to fake a poker face. There's one thing my friends and family know about me: I can't lie. I don't have a poker face. I never have. It is a blessing and a curse, but I would rather be brutally honest and non-sugar coated instead of a total kiss-ass, or a fake lil' you know what.

Am I great at organizing, streamlining, systematizing, automating, and decluttering? Why yes, yes, I am. Cue the start of Let's Get You Organized. I employed four women during that season of my life. We served over *two hundred and fifty* clients in creating lifestyle changes to help local families live more efficient lives.

When the physical decluttering thing didn't do it for me anymore, I pivoted to Online Business Management, working as a Virtual Assistant for over twenty small businesses. And when that well dried up, I gathered my resources and connections, searched long and hard (ahem... over 500 applications, 50 interviews, 25 final stages, and 2 offers) and landed a job as the Executive Assistant to the CEO of an amazing startup. By zeroing in on my strengths, I was able to find the perfect role, boss, and company *for me*.

Stay in your own lane. Focus on your own sht. Get clear on what you're good at. Block out the rest.

For extra credit here, you could dive into the multitude of free online personality tests which from a sociological standpoint (my Bachelor of Arts degree is in Sociology, by the way, Magna Cum Laude say whattt), can give you a great indicator of your next best position. The Myers-Briggs Type Indicator, Enneagram, DISC, CliftonStrengths, and Human Design are all easy and free (or incredibly cheap) tools to help you figure out your next move. Because without knowing yourself first, how can you even *begin* to choose from the wide variety of open jobs in your area? Home in on those natural skills and abilities and suddenly you can start to see where you fit into the larger puzzle of life.

"The definition of insanity is doing the same thing over and over again and expecting different results."

-No, it's not by Albert Einstein (or Ben Franklin) but it's an impactful anonymous quote nonetheless

So at this point, you are hopefully starting to see the patterns of your super-cool negative-story-writing abilities, your ability to focus on your weaknesses like no other, your excuses holding you back from discovering your true passion(s), and your awesome way of listening to every doubter that crosses your path. Fun stuff, right? Buckle up. We're just getting started.

Pivoting with Purpose Tip

Stop focusing on the sht that you KNOW you're never going to change about yourself. Embrace your natural gifts, talents, and abilities instead. Those are already your strengths, and now you need to up your game and show yourself a little love to be able to step into that full-blown badass that you already know you are!

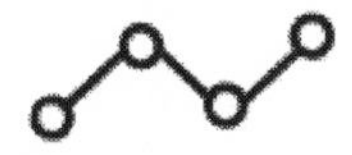

Chapter 4:

Passion Over Paychecks

But seriously, I hope you can see all the crap that is keeping you stuck so you can start to hammer away at it like a determined little woodpecker. Remember at the beginning of this book when I told you I was making six figures at the age of 28? And how I realized that money doesn't buy happiness? Let's revisit that.

See, being able to work in that sweet spot of the Venn diagram where you can do what you're really good at and also get paid for it, is the goal for many. For me, living in that sweet spot has brought more alignment and happiness into my life than I could ever imagine. It is true role alignment and purpose alignment at work. I might not be making as much *money* by taking the steps to work in a field that lights me up every day, but I am sure as hell more emotionally, spiritually, and mentally *wealthy*. That is the beauty of following your passion, not a paycheck.

I started my second business, Let's Get You Hired, because I saw SO many of my friends and colleagues staying unhappy in jobs they hated. Some were grasping at straws, trying to hold on to a role that kept them crying in cubicles, or lashing out at their partners every evening. Others were playing it safe in the rat race, at a job that was "just fine," living that "good enough" life, and letting their passions die within them.

Not loving what you do at work? Paycheck feels like an empty obligation or burden? That probably feels like a whole lot of resentment for your boss, your coworkers, and your job in general.

Without the fuel of excitement and fiery motivation to go through the hard times, the paycheck at the end of a long, grueling, month won't matter. I'm all about aligning your passions with your paycheck- focus on your passions first, paycheck second.

And while you're at it, stop sending mixed messages about what you want and what lights you up. No good comes out of mixed messages — in your relationships, in your emails, in your texts to ex-boyfriends, or in the requests / thoughts / prayers / manifestations that you send up to the job search gods. Once you are clear on what types of jobs you want to apply for, in the cities you'd love to live in, with the type of boss or coworkers you would love to work with, at the type of company that aligns with your personal values, that is where the real magic happens.

If you intend to move to Philly and start working in Public Relations for an eco-conscious brand that is women-founded and quickly growing in the startup community, then hop on over to LinkedIn and start your search. If you intend to move to Portland and start working in Recruiting for a national chain of successful agencies with an LGBTQ+ friendly environment, then get on Indeed, Glassdoor, Monster, or even good ole Craigslist to find your match. Don't get stuck in thinking it must be a typical 9-5 type job, either. There are plenty of positions for part-time creatives, out-of-the-box thinkers that want to work remotely, and night owls that prefer overnight shifts.

Get *targeted* in your search just like you would in an online dating setting. Only like dudes that are over six feet tall? You would create a filter. Allergic to cats? You would create a filter for your dream guy sans kitties. Want an older man? You would adjust the age settings. Think about how much targeted time you have spent on online dating apps over the years. Then think about how much targeted time you have put into your job search! See the difference? Filter it up, get strategic, and follow your true passions. No more mixed messages. Write out *exactly* what you want and give the world a chance to open up to you.

Pivoting with Purpose Tip

Find out what you are good at- you're not getting any younger. Stop sending mixed messages and let the universe do its thing.

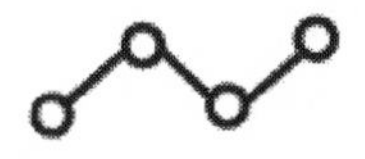

Chapter 5:

Your Path, Your Journey

Although I know where my zone of greatness is and therefore have this huge massive vision for my life (hello, keynote speeches for stadiums of thousands in the audience), I still have no clue *how* I'm going to get there. But here's the thing, it's not about knowing the *how*. If you can pinpoint the how then it is not *your* journey.

When I was crying in my gray cubicle over the twat boss, I couldn't have even *dreamed* of where I would be in three years, let alone one year, or even six months. I had the vision for myself that I would leave my 9-5 and go full time with my side hustle at Let's Get You Organized. That's it.

I had no idea how I would make enough money to replace my salary (or even a livable wage, for that matter). I had enough savings for one year, so my backup plan was to get a job if the business failed (or if I failed at business). I had the financial safety net in place (and a fear mindset that was about just as big). Leaving a 9-5 without having a fully lucrative side hustle was *terrifying*. But at least it was a starting point.

Within a few months of launching the LLC, I had clients booked out for months in advance and eventually made my first hire. During that first year in business, awesome movement would happen and then I would move to the next step. Another win would come in, and I would take another step forward. Sht would hit the fan and blow me backward, but I would get back up and keep running. One. Step. At. A. Time.

Two years later, my business had been featured on over twenty-five podcasts, I was paid to speak on fifteen stages, and I had written for twenty-some-odd nationally published articles in the likes of Market Watch, Amex Business Blog, Spectrum Business Insights, and even contributed a chapter to a best-selling book. How the hell did all of that happen? Because I just. took. the. next. step. See, it is not about the *how*. It is about making sht happen and making progress every single day.

"A little progress every day adds up to big results."
- Satya Nani

If you know the exact next step because you are following someone else's blueprint, then guess what? It's not your journey. There is no magic pill. There is no quick fix. There is no five-step formula. It is *your* journey, and it is going to play out however it is meant to. There is power in knowing that you are co-creating your life's journey at all times.

Pivoting with Purpose Tip

Not happy in your current role? Burnt the eff out, trying to make it as an entrepreneur? Switch things up. Take a sidestep in a new direction. See what magic lies outside that comfort zone, because on the other side is your zone of *greatness*.

Chapter 6:

Action Cures Fear

Ever heard of the term "analysis paralysis?" Ahh yes, everyone's favorite conundrum of being stuck on the fence. The funny thing about just taking the next step is it provides this wonderful thing called *clarity*. Clarity is *key* as you navigate your job search journey.

When you interview at a company that doesn't feel good, you might learn more about what you're *not* looking for (in the dating world, that equates to the whole "kissing frogs" metaphor).

If you take the steps to land a phone interview for a job in a new city, you might realize that you have it pretty good where you're at (cost of living and all)!

When you muster up the courage to apply to roles in a field you have never worked in before, you can expand your comfort zone and start to reframe your mindset of what is possible.

Baby steps work.
I am a firm believer that action cures fear. Take the leap. Start today. By getting your butt off the couch, your eyes turned away from Netflix, and your mind off of the fridge that calls to you 24/7, you can carve out the time to focus on the activities that move your job search *forward*.

Clear the clutter by setting boundaries and saying "no" to non-ideal jobs, recruiters, and hiring managers.

If you have been kissing frogs lately, then it is probably time to re-identify your ideal role, culture, location, team, and working style so that you can *stop* attracting non-ideal positions. Make a list of the past roles that you have absolutely *loved*, then identify three to five traits they have in common. This will give you a roadmap to the *exact* types of companies and teams you want to work with and cut out the desperation of saying "yes" to anyone and everyone!

I am not one of those people that says, "Treat your job search like it is your full-time job." Because let's face it, that is unrealistic. There are funemployment brunches to be had, beach trips to be taken, and Netflix series to binge.

But I *am* one of those people that says you must make a little progress *every single day* to see results. Start with just twenty minutes of journaling and self-reflection. Build up to twenty minutes of journaling + twenty minutes of resume updating. Then add on another twenty minutes of personality testing. And from there, you may just be off to visit the hiring gods!

See, it's a lot like working out. You are not going to visit a personal trainer on day one at your new gym and say, "I want to be a bodybuilder tomorrow." Just like you are not going to find your ultimate purpose or your dream job overnight. It takes *time and effort*. By starting small and implementing daily lifestyle changes, you can surely hit your goal of landing that perfect position.

Stop trying to take the shortcuts. Start living your purpose and vision. It is time to take the leap to what you truly want in life!

Take the leap and see where the net appears.

When you start to take action, you may start to notice little whispers here and there, like that slight sound of a door creaking open somewhere. It might be a friend in New York City that *coincidentally* has the coveted role of "Roommate" coming up, just when your lease in Boringtown USA ends. It might be a family member in Seattle that owns a business and emails you about needing to hire someone *just like you*. Or it might be an old LinkedIn acquaintance that makes a post which gives you a lightbulb idea moment to launch you into your next targeted job application. There is always a net, you just have to open your eyes enough to see it.

Pivoting with Purpose Tip

Get out of analysis-paralysis mode and start kissing some frogs. Play in the damn puddle and get your feet wet! Oh, and get off the fence, that is an *uncomfortable* place to be.

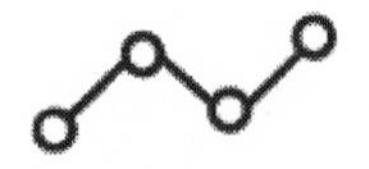

Chapter 7:

Get Your Shift Together

I miscarried right before leaving the twat boss job, we called off the wedding, and I moved out. Oof. Sounds tough right? It was. Really tough.

But I grew from it. Immensely. When I realized that I was settling and not giving myself what I truly wanted, I knew it was time to go.

When I first started the journey to "finding myself" (I hate that term btw) I knew the relationship I was in was not serving me. We attended many couples therapy sessions, experienced the super fun on again/off again vicious breakup cycle, and I was engaged, pregnant, and living in my dream white picket fence home before truly calling the relationship quits.

You may ask, why would I ruin such a good thing? Why would I opt out of a life that most would dream of? Because I was settling for a life that was *good enough* and I knew we wouldn't last.

I was feeling stuck in my life after meeting the person I thought was going to be my partner forever and then quickly became unfulfilled.

I was feeling stuck in my life after getting a puppy, seeing my childhood traumas of emotional neglect play out while parenting that puppy, then rehoming him, and deciding that I am most likely not going to raise children in this lifetime.

I was feeling stuck in my life after launching a business, but still not understanding how to operate outside of corporate life.

I was feeling stuck in my life after having small snippet visions of my greatness, but not having a clue how I would break through the heavy ceiling I had created for myself.

I was feeling stuck in my life churning around in my little hamster wheel of insanity, doing the same things over and over again and expecting a different result.

And then I decided to level up.

I hired my very first coach. I was an athlete my whole life and had gymnastics coaches, soccer coaches, softball coaches, CrossFit coaches, personal trainers, and a bazillion therapists. But what the hell was a "life coach?" Well, for one thing, she charged $2,000 per month to work with her. She lived across the country. She only chatted with me through text on Facebook Live in her group (she showed up on video while group members typed in questions). And we never even talked on the phone! But I invested anyway.

I felt crazy. Like the only thing I'd ever spent $6,000 on was a *car*. I was in my 20s. Who the hell did I think I was, dropping half my savings on some random person that I would never even meet?

But it felt so aligned in my soul. Every cell in my body knew that she was the coach for me.

I had searched a random Facebook group with the term "coach" and her name was recommended there. I clicked on her website, watched a webinar, scheduled a call with someone on her team, and the next day I transferred $6,000 from my PayPal account to her bank account.

“What the hell are you doing?!"

My ego was having an existential crisis. But again, I felt this peaceful, calm, nudging voice from my soul that this was the right path. That was the very first time I let my soul win. I pushed my ego to the curb and did something in alignment with my *soul.* Talk about an unfamiliar experience.

If I hadn't invested a big scary amount in her ninety-day program, I wouldn't have skin in the game. I wouldn't have shown up for myself. It would just be another "free challenge" or "e-book" or "spiritual journaling prompt" that I would opt in to and never use. You know, the ones that collect dust in your email inbox (or worse, printed out paper clutter). But I invested $6,000. I took the scary leap.

And guess what? I hit every single goal I set out to hit that year in both my business and personal life. I was a non-believer for so long, seeing "life coach this" and "mentor that" everywhere. That sweet feeling of success is out there waiting for you. It's okay to ask for help along the way.

Break down to breakthrough.
What about that old closet of skeletons? Oh yea, those need to be cleaned out too. Most likely, there's some emotional baggage that needs to be released before you can opt into that big massive vision you have for your life.

If you feel like you have tried every medication out there, read every self-help book on the shelf, attended every yoga class and meditation session, and you *still* feel haunted by your damn childhood or relationship or insert-whatever-here trauma, then... *it's time to call in the big guns.*

It could be cognitive behavioral therapy, EMDR therapy, hypnosis, past-life regression sessions, going to a weeklong retreat, engaging in a weekend seminar, or maybe even an ayahuasca trip down in

Southern America. Now, I'm no doctor or psychiatrist so let's not get this twisted, but over the years of helping my fellow millennials find their gift to move into the future and simultaneously let go of their past, I know it can take some creative problem solving and innovative thinking to let it go. Cue Elsa.

Release your emotional baggage and set yourself free from those anchors that have been chaining you down. When you feel those triggers getting you down, pretend you have giant chain clippers in your hands and visualize yourself going "snip, snip, snip" until you feel free again. Others might just need to scream that catchy song from 'Frozen.'

But hold please, just a second. You might have some physical clutter to clear away first. This isn't necessarily the fun stuff, but before you can see results, you've got to get some things in order.

Pivoting with Purpose Tip

You probably need therapy. But you probably already knew that. Kick your ego to the curb and stop letting your ugly old suitcase full of skeletons hold you back from the big massive vision you have for your life.

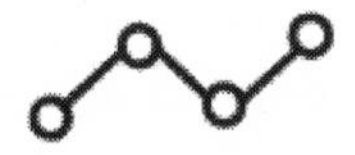

Chapter 8:

Clear the Clutter

By staying organized in your job search, you may not only get a job faster, but you can also become a better manager of your time, money, and energy. Because let's face it, the job market is like the Wild Wild West and you need to be prepared to handle it.

If you have ever taken an anatomy class, then you have seen the incredible efficiency of the human body's operating system. It is *amazing* to see the massive amount of perfect systems, processes, and workflows that occur second by second within us! So how the heck can humans survive in the twenty-first century, with all sorts of distractions and clutter weighing us down?

My calendar looks like a color-coded, time blocked, game of Tetris.

I have a to-do list even on weekends. I have been called hyper, fiery, and feisty my whole life and I have been referred to as the Energizer Bunny, the Tasmanian Devil, and Mighty Mouse by multiple people in multiple different situations.

Why am I like this? Well for starters, I was diagnosed with obsessive-compulsive disorder at age nine. I grew up in a hoarding household with a father that was a saver and a packrat that filled our home with tons of stuff. If a container of yogurt was eaten, you better believe he was going to reuse it "someday." If a box was emptied, he would add it to that floor-to-ceiling pile in the garage.

Remember my alphabetizing magazines story? My brother had quite a fun time with headgear, retainers, rubber bands, braces, and the whole dental-nine-yards as a kid. I spent plenty of time in the waiting room. But my organized and productive nature wouldn't let me sit idly still. Instead, I took it upon myself to gather up and alphabetize *every single magazine* in that dental office. To the surprise and delight of the dentist and his staff, I will never live that story down! Plus, I have fond memories of organizing my mom's craft closet on weekends or front facing the condiments in my aunt's refrigerator, if that tells you anything about me.

Fast forward to age 21 when I first launched my professional home organizing business with just a blog, cheap business cards, and a few Craigslist ads. By age 28, I left the twat boss job and helped *tons* of disorganized clients in their homes.

There was Melanie, who was hanging on to all of her wedding pictures, albums, VHS tapes, even her bouquet from a marriage that had ended *ten years* prior. An empty-nester, she was burnt out at her job and had a nagging feeling that all of her crap was holding her back from stepping into the next stage of her life. After working with me, her statement of feeling so much "lighter" and noting that my decluttering service was *life-changing* felt like the best payment in the world.

Then there was Eileen, who desperately wanted to "Marie Kondo" her life before going back to work after being a stay-at-home-mom for five years. Throughout *fifteen sessions*, I worked with her to remove over *ten truckfuls* and *three dumpsters* of stuff from her cluttered home. What do you think happened after that major lifestyle change? She cleared the clutter to make room for the next opportunity to come through. And it did! Eileen landed a six-figure job working for an attorney within a few months.

Become an energy-efficient human.
Stop letting all your power go to waste like Melanie and Eileen. I have found that just a few simple tips and tricks introduced into your daily life can make a huge impact on your sanity during a job search.

If you are cluttered and disorganized or your life feels chaotic, as if it is not structured or streamlined like the well-oiled and energy-efficient human-machine, then this chapter is for you. If you have goals to become a minimalist, get organized, manage time effectively, and be more productive, then this chapter is for you too. Before you can re-enter the workforce, it's time to make sure your home base is in order first.

Are you ready to save time in your day-to-day activities and save money on not buying so much stuff? Are you ready to tackle your clutter, stop the madness on your over-scheduled calendar, and finally have time in the day to work out, study for that next degree or certification, or spend more time with your family? Are you ready to feel successful, productive, and as if your life works as autonomously as your organs do?

I fully believe that YOU can be an energy-efficient human.

Our environments are an outer reflection of our inner state. When our minds are cluttered, our desks, homes, cars, and everything else becomes cluttered! Breaking long-standing habits can be tough work, but it is important work to be done. Change your habits and change your life. If you're stressed about money and finding a new job, then your home probably shows physical signs of that stress.

Your home is solace from the outside world, your nest. Clearing your clutter requires giving yourself room to grow mentally, physically, and emotionally. Imagine the day you got your keys to your office or your new home. What emotions were you filled with? What were the sights, sounds, and feelings you had at this time in your life? What emotions do you have about your environment now? What was your vision for that space before you filled it with a bunch of stuff? Usually, the words that came to mind are excitement, peacefulness, accomplishment, pride, or a sense of security. It is time to get you back to that place!

If you feel like you constantly hold on to sentimental clutter, like old photos of ex-boyfriends, or souvenirs from trips with friends that are long gone then ask yourself: Am I keeping this or buying this to fill a deep emotional void within me? Am I holding on to this piece of clutter or buying this item because I'm living in the "somedays" and "what ifs"? Am I in analysis-paralysis and don't know how to start the decluttering process?

If the answer is yes to these questions, then it is time to do some soul searching and discover the source of those emotional voids! You could hire a local professional organizer, coach, or therapist to help you through these emotions and get you back on track to a more organized life. Go into your next job with clarity, peace of mind, and a calm place to rest your head at night.

Minimalism is totally trending.

Ever felt like things are out of control in your life? Not sure where to start on your journey to a more productive and simple way of living? Do you want to stop living in fear of not having enough? A scarcity mindset can be a real a**hole when we're already in a state of transition in our careers and our lives.

The Baby Boomers are aging, and they are still holding on to "generational clutter" from their parents that grew up during America's Great Depression. Hoarders, packrats, savers. The minimalist generation is changing all of that. We have so much *stuff* as Americans — the latest iPhone, the fancy new car, the trends from the mall, the newest skincare product, the latest tech gadget. Over the years, I have seen my clients feel totally overwhelmed by the amount of stuff lurking around their home. Maybe you have recently experienced an avalanche in the hall closet and found war in the kitchen cabinets!

Have you ever noticed that we, as humans, have *so much* difficulty letting go of things that we never use?

It is *so* important to regularly purge our items to clear space and leave room for new energy and new opportunities. It is time to make fast decisions on what to keep and what to toss so you can get past the cluttered chaos! Make your life *simpler* with *less stuff*. Live life with *less* so you can enjoy life *more*! Decluttering has this amazing way of making life a lot more manageable, especially when we're in times of transition and already feel weighed down. Let's get you on the path to owning less crap and simplifying your life.

For those that are just starting their journey to a minimalist life, I recommend starting small and setting a timer for twenty minutes in a non-emotional area such as the medicine cabinet, spice rack, car's glove box, or nightstand. Decluttering can be overwhelming so it's important to take baby steps and gain momentum! Get rid of what you no longer need and feel the weight lifted off your shoulders.

Happy home, happy job search.
Oh, and have any of you heard about this idea of *decision fatigue*? Our brains are only wired to be able to make a certain amount of decisions each day, so it is super important that we minimize the number of decisions we are forcing our brains to make! Incorporating a capsule wardrobe into your life means only having a select few pieces of clothing in your closet — instead of piles of clothes everywhere and not being able to figure out an outfit quickly when getting ready in the morning.

It sounds like Mark Zuckerberg, Steve Jobs, and Barack Obama are on to something.

You can also minimize your calendar obligations by choosing to attend the appointments and events that are absolutely necessary to your career growth so that you can make room for what matters. Say no. Set boundaries. Stick to a schedule. Clear the calendar clutter!

Find a designated desk space for your job search, stat! Sure, it could be a kitchen table, a dine-in bar, or even your coffee table while sitting cross-legged on the floor.

Just like there's something to be said for getting out of your PJs and putting on "real clothes" while job hunting, there's also something to be said about computing from a clean flat surface that is not your lap. Set yourself up for success.

If your desk or computer desktop looks like a bomb hit it, then try strategically labeling digital files and physical items in your home and office. Labels help our brain identify items much more quickly than trying to search through our mental database. Imagine the last time you had to go through lists and lists of files on the computer to find something you were looking for, or maybe a time you had to sift through tons of bins or boxes in your garage when it was time to decorate for holidays. You were probably left feeling frustrated, and like you were wasting time. For years, I have been helping my clients keep file naming conventions to a set of standards where we have labeled items in the pantry, closet, garage, and other high traffic areas, and I can tell you- *labels work!*

Pivoting with Purpose Tip
Get your calendar in order, designate a desk space, and clean your damn house.

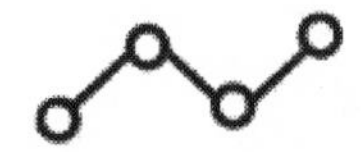

Chapter 9:

Prioritization and Procrastination

Once your space is clear (and your mind too), you can make room to focus on the needle movers in your job search. There's no force of momentum like getting a big win, so let's try to rack up more of those!

It is super easy to get lost in the sea of jobs out there. If you do not have your proverbial ducks in a row, things could get messy when your phone starts ringing. When I worked as a temp placement recruiter, I had multiple candidates call me by the wrong name or think they were applying to a job with a different company, and some didn't even remember the job that they had applied for in the first place! Not a good look. Keep track of your progress and store all the details in one central place. Ideally, not your already overcrowded brain.

If you are more of a digital tracker, hop on to Excel (or if you can't afford Microsoft Office Suite, then hop on over to your Gmail account and log in to your free Google Drive, where the Google version called 'Sheets' lives). In either the paper or digital tracker, you can map out all the jobs you have applied to thus far including company names, recruiter or hiring manager names, position, date applied, and other pertinent details. You can also use that same workbook to track which companies are in your area, which companies align with your values, which companies have the types of benefits you need (like working from home, a flexible schedule, casual environment, company 401k match or contribution, medical/dental/vision) and use that as your daily guide to mapping out your next prospects.

"What gets measured, gets improved."

-Peter Drucker

If you want to further track how you are moving the needle forward in your job search every single day, one simple hack is to write it down! If you are a pen and paper type of person, grab a new notebook to designate as your job search planner or tracker. It doesn't have to be a $30 ridiculously elaborate planner; it could be something as simple as a 79-cent old-school composition book. Jot down one to three items that moved the needle forward every day. Try it first thing in the morning or mark it as the last thing before you go to bed. This trains your brain to notice the little things and also motivates you to be productive if you find yourself in that 3 pm slump and not feeling driven to make progress. I recommend grabbing a new notebook, labeling it your Progress Tracker, and start moving that needle forward!

Now that you have your designated workspace and your designated job search tracker, there's more organization to do — I know, don't hate me. But let's keep it simple. For starters, do not name your resume "Resume.doc". Take the time to put in your First and Last name and save it as a PDF for a more polished and professional look. Organize your digital files so that you have a special spot for your resume, cover letter, and other credential documents.

Back in my recruiting days, I once had a candidate attach something that, let's just say was completely humiliating and embarrassing to the point where after trying to recall the message, he ended up just falling off the face of the earth entirely! Don't make that mistake. File naming conventions are important!

Clean it up! (said in my best Orbitz gum girl Australian accent).

You may also want to clear the clutter on your digital footprint. Those old keg stand photos that are marked "Public" on your Facebook profile page? Mark 'em "Private" (or delete them altogether, sheesh). That YouTube video you filmed ten years ago when you decided to represent a failed multi-level marketing (MLM) company? Unpublish it or change your name and handle to not list your real name. Those Reddit comments spouting off your religious or political views? Hide 'em. All it takes is a simple Google search with less than desirable results for a recruiter or hiring manager to toss your resume into the Recycle Bin. Technically, hiring managers should not be poking around your personal life, but if you are making it easy to find all those skeletons in your closet, then can you even blame them?

Move the needle forward.

Let me tell you a little bit about the 80/20 Rule, also known as "The Pareto Principle." There was an Italian guy in the late 1800s that decided Economics was his jam. Specifically, data and statistics really got him going. He said that 20% of our effort leads to 80% of our results. In a job search context, that means that 20% of your activities are going to lead to 80% of your achieved goals. You know, like phone screens, returned LinkedIn messages, callbacks, Zoom sessions, and the ever-so-coveted in-person interview opportunities.

Do you know what is moving the needle forward in your search for the next best job? Is it doubling down on writing original LinkedIn content through articles and infographics to share with your network? Or attending virtual networking events and personally branding yourself on a platform like Instagram or Twitter? Could it be creating a YouTube channel that highlights your expertise in your field and helps you to engage with potential hiring managers via curated video content?

Figure out what is getting you positive results and cut out the rest of the fluff.

A quick way to discover your sweet spot of the 20% needle movers is to take out a piece of paper and a pen, draw a cross down the middle, place your recent "Wins" on the left side, and your recent "Tasks" on the right side. Once you've listed out several in each category, draw a line from your Win to the Task that helped you achieve it. Starting to see a pattern? You may notice that there are *multiple* wins tied to only a *few* tasks. That is where you can double down. Those tasks are your game changers!

Maybe the 80/20 rule is not for you, and if it isn't then let's try a SWOT analysis. Turn that piece of paper over and draw another cross on the back. Then place one of these words in each quadrant: Strengths. Weaknesses. Opportunities. Threats.

Strengths: Remember to focus on your strengths, gifts, talents, purpose, and natural abilities. What are you really freaking good at? What are you known for amongst your friends and family?

Weaknesses: On the flipside, what do you know that you're probably never going to be good at? Remember my account of knowing that I'm not patient, diplomatic, or poised? I am fully aware that I am probably not going to change anytime soon!

Opportunities: What has been coming into your pipeline lately? Are you seeing those "coincidences" come through? Remember the family member reaching out, or the friend offering up a room, or other little whispers from the universe.

Threats: It could be the current unemployment rate in your area. Or maybe you have been out of the workforce for quite a while (or never even had a "real job" to begin with) and you are worried there may be a ton of competition out there. You know, like those *without* any huge job gaps in their resume progression. Write out three to five items in each quadrant and let that be your guide to start going about your job search *strategically.* Stop throwing spaghetti at the wall, hoping something will stick! It's time to get strategic.

Pivoting with Purpose Tip
Track your progress, call in the SWOT team, and clean up that dusty old digital footprint because it's time to get organized, clear, and focused. You know, like *adulting*.

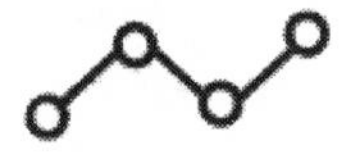

Chapter 10:

Girls Got Goals

The truth is, I couldn't have gotten out of my job funk without staying organized, goal setting, managing time effectively, and prioritizing my daily to-dos. But before we get down to the nitty-gritty of your strategic job search, let's get clear on a few things.

Are you worried that you're a "sellout" if you didn't make it in a particular industry or decided you hated a certain field? Are you hoping that a staffing agency recruiter will solve all of your problems? Do you feel like you need to go back to school for ABC Certification or XYZ Degree before you can land the job of your dreams? Do you know what you truly *value*, both personally and professionally?

You're not a sellout for deciding to move on from something that is no longer serving you. There is a reason for every season and like Gary Vaynerchuck always says, looking back will only hurt your neck.

As a little kid, I used to be so concerned about wearing the same thing twice in two weeks... as if people actually paid enough attention to me and cared enough to mentally note what I was wearing each day, and then turn around and judge me for it. The same theme crept into my business life when I was afraid to repurpose social media content that had already been posted six months ago... as if anyone would even remember what I posted six months ago, let alone six weeks ago! We all tend to care *so much* about what other people think. Even as adults.

Hopefully, by this point in the book, you have already started your journey of quieting the doubters, but now it's time to quiet your inner doubt monster. This might sound harsh, but no one cares as much as you think they do. When I left my life as a full-time entrepreneur, I thought all my business-owner friends would disown me. Instead, I received message after message with my network asking me how I got my shiny new job and how they could get one too. Rewrite the story that you're a sellout and move on to bigger and better ways of thinking! The bitter reality is that honestly, no one is paying attention.

Agencies are not for the faint of heart.
A staffing agency is usually *not* the answer. Staffing agency recruiters work in very strict guidelines called job requisitions. They are paid by their *clients*, not by you. That means that their black and white job requisitions are created by the company that is hiring and usually requires *very* specific skill sets to fill the role. That is why companies don't just post the job themselves — they outsource to a staffing agency to help find that "purple unicorn" candidate that may or may not exist!

When you enter a recruiting agency, you need to be on point. You need to know exactly who you are, who you serve, what you do, what salary you are looking for, and where you want to be (on an org chart *and* in a geographical location). If you go into one of these cutthroat agencies feeling timid, shy, scared, or confused, chances are you're not going to get to the top of their pile. I always recommend working with a career coach or career transition consultant *first* before working with a staffing agency.

Many times, there are temporary placements that may hold you over for a little while financially, but they are not long-term positions and are usually a "churn and burn" type role with high turnover. To me, that sounds like living a life that is just *good enough*. By this point, you should know that I am not a fan of that kind of life!

Real life experience trumps education. Stop accruing student loan debt. Start getting experience. You don't need another acronym or abbreviation after your name on your resume or LinkedIn profile. Recruiters want to see real, tangible experience, not just academic success. In the past when I was a recruiter at a staffing agency, I would cringe at the resumes where all an applicant had was a master's degree and a bunch of on-campus college experience volunteering here and there.

The 9-5 world is no joke. When I would have a job req in front of me, staring me down with a deadline and a due date for my client to hire someone new, I would always want to make sure the candidates I represented were emotionally intelligent, great collaborators, knew how to build teams, and could communicate effectively. Many times, those with their nose in a book and no real-life experience had let me down in these areas. Just like a Pavlov dog, I quickly learned that when I placed candidates with tons of "boots on the ground" experience, my successful placement rate would go up. That meant more money in my pocket and more happy employees for my clients. It was a no-brainer that the money was in those candidates with valuable experience, not just a bunch of expensive schooling.

Ask yourself if you're just stalling or procrastinating by telling yourself you need to go back to school. You may be avoiding the job applications and resume writing because you are too scared to take the plunge into the job market! Dig deeper into why you're telling yourself that story.

"Values are like fingerprints. Nobody's are the same, but you leave 'em all over everything you do."

-Elvis Presley

My current values are freedom, power, and community. I never want to work in the strict confines of a rigid box or have a micromanager on my back because I want the freedom to be creative and express myself at work! I need to feel like my ideas matter, like I can contribute important information to my boss or my team, and like I have a certain level of decision-making power.

When I realized I didn't want to work for another Fortune 500 company ever again, I found my groove in the startup world. Startups provided me with that feeling of flexibility that I *crave*. I also need to feel like I have a sense of power in deciding how my day will run, which is why work-from-home roles tend to work best for me. And I need to feel like I have a sense of community around me — whether that is holding webinars for our clients, or hosting networking events, or speaking on stage at live workshops and conferences. I discovered that I place inherent value on these three buckets and without them, I am not a very happy employee!

"Life isn't about finding yourself. Life is about creating yourself."
-George Bernard Shaw

What are your values? What do you *need* to be able to feel happy and fulfilled at work?

You might need to slow down to speed up. By taking a step back to look at the bigger picture, you can have clarity when diving into your hunt for the best job. The 80/20 Rule Activity, SWOT Analysis, and Excel/Google Sheet tracker are all great ways to slow down, get strategic, and get clear — but let's review a few more!

The sands of time.

Back in the day, there was a university professor who came into the class with an empty glass jar. He filled the jar with a bunch of sand and asked his students if the jar was full. Well yea, duh. It was. But then he poured the sand out and put some pebbles in, then the sand. Is it full now? Oh crap, it just got fuller! And then he dumped it out again and placed a few big rocks in, then pebbles, then sand.

Get it? There is always room for more if you are strategic about what you place in your jar. Think of your jar as your day. Every day you get a new empty jar and it's up to you what will go into it. Time management is crucial to your success in landing the perfect job. Filling up your day with lots of sand makes it so that your big rocks are unable to fit into your day.

Big rocks first, sand second! For a job seeker, rocks may be networking calls, phone screens, in-person interviews, resume overhauls, or writing a new cover letter.

Pebbles could be creating a LinkedIn post, grabbing coffee with an old coworker to get a pulse on the current job market, or setting up new tech for yourself to ramp up your job search from home.

Sandy activities could include scrolling social media and getting "comparisonitis" over all the amazing things people seem to be doing, hanging out with people that are not where you want to be in life or people that are not doing things that you want to be doing in life, or attending events with no real return on investment of your time, money, or energy.

What are the sandy activities that are weighing you down? Start focusing on the big rocks of your day! It can take *months* to find and land the perfect role for you. Ask yourself: "Am I in this for the long game?" Don't get burnt out during the warmup!

To help you figure out those big rocks go ahead and start making your goals SMARTER. You have probably heard of S.M.A.R.T. goals by now- the idea of avoiding non-specific goals by breaking them up into bite-sized chunks that are Specific, Measurable, Achievable/ Attainable, Relevant/Realistic, & Timely. But have you been to the ER lately? Evaluate & Re-adjust.

Many times, we don't hit the ambitious goals that we set out to achieve. That is precisely the right time to take a look back at your progress, figure out what worked and what didn't, and then go back to the drawing board.

If I go to lunch with a friend and tell her "I want to lose weight." Is that a S.M.A.R.T. goal? No. If I tell my friend "I want to lose thirty pounds within ninety days and I am going to hire a personal trainer, weigh myself once per week, and outsource my nutrition to an awesome local organic meal prep company," that sounds a lot more S.M.A.R.T. right? But what happens when I hit day sixty and I realize I have only lost ten pounds? The reality is I am probably not going to lose twenty more pounds in that final month (unless I develop a drug habit or get sick... no thanks). That is the best time to make the goal even *smarter,* by evaluating and readjusting.

"A goal without a plan is just a wish."
-Antoine de Saint-Exupéry

If your goal is to land your dream job, boss, team, and company, then it is time to start setting your goals around what that is going to look like and how you are going to make it happen! You may have also heard of KPIs, also known as Key Performance Indicators. By setting certain triggers of how you measure your success, you can see what is working and what is not.

Many times, job seekers achieve a win, but they never really look back at what moved the needle. Evaluation and analysis are *crucial* when looking at what is driving the biggest results for you. Once identified, you can shift and pivot your plan to continue to work towards the end goal of landing your perfect role!

I love to ask myself daily, "What are three actions I could do today that will move me closer to my big scary goal?"

No more throwing spaghetti at the wall,
no more scurrying around a hamster wheel,
no more becoming a rat the race. You're better than that!

Pivoting with Purpose Tip

Find your values, set those goals, figure out your needle-movers, and manage your time like a boss. You got this. I believe in you!

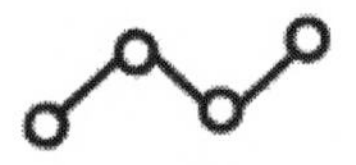

Chapter 11:

Your Network is Your Net Worth

Be prepared to talk about yourself! Do you have an elevator pitch? I like to sum up what I do best in ten words or less. That way when you are asked that dreaded question, "What do you do?" at a networking event, you can easily recite your memorized statement! Think of it as your personal branding statement that you can tie into your LinkedIn profile, your resume headline, or even use it as a tagline on your business cards! "Hi, I'm ____ and I help ___ with ____" usually does the trick. Keep it short and to the point! Make it funny or memorable.

Your elevator pitch is your lead into longer 1:1 interactions that build the know-like-trust factor. People have to get to *know* you, so don't be afraid to be vulnerable, funny, your true weird self, or showcase your values and what is important to you! Find a relatable subject that is common ground for the two of you when speaking with each other. Do they have kids? Are they married? Are they from a foreign country? Do they have a degree in the same field as you? Figure out something the two of you have in common and you can become instantly more *likable*. They need to *trust* you to give up a business card or phone number or LinkedIn connection.

Look people in the eye. Remember people's names. Be sincere in referring other people to them or jotting down their info to meet at a later date. Bring a friend or colleague with you if you're nervous or shy at in-person events. Listen more than you speak. Have business cards on you, or if you are not currently with a company then order cheapie personal cards from an online provider like Vistaprint. Better yet, whip out your phone and connect with them on LinkedIn right then and there!

"The richest people in the world look for and build networks; everyone else looks for work."
-Robert Kiyosaki

Amid *five hundred* applications, I kept track of all of my touchpoints in my handy dandy Google Sheets doc (aka the free version of Excel) and figured out that it was more about connecting with those warm leads versus trying to blanket the entire digital earth with my resume.

Sending out hundreds of parsed resumes to funky Applicant Tracking Systems (ATS) never worked for me. I kicked those ATS bots to the curb and made *human* connections by grabbing coffee with new people that were friends of friends or reaching out to old coworkers and fellow university alumni. How did I land my dream job after being out of the game for several years? Well, I had interviewed with someone *eight years* prior at a large firm and stayed in touch with her via LinkedIn, only to see that she had launched her own company and now, all of these years later, she was looking to add new employees to her team! That is the true magic of networking and using social platforms to foster connections with others in your industry.

Pivoting with Purpose Tip

Whether it is in-person networking events, virtual conferences, Zoom Happy Hours, or breakout sessions during a webinar, it's time to learn how to talk yourself up, grow your network, and make genuine connections with those around you. Whoever first said, "It is all about who you *know*" was damn right!

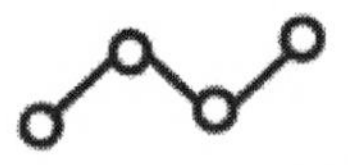

Chapter 12: Competence is Confidence

Now that you have networked your little heart out and learned how to build that know-like-trust factor with potential job prospects, let's speed up your job search using the tactics and strategies I have learned along the way.

Upgrade your resume, upgrade your life. First things first- aesthetics are *everything*. That black and white Times New Roman resume you learned how to make in high school is not going to get you anywhere! Update it with personally branded templates in easy-to-use online platforms like Canva. Choose your colors, add in a headshot (or a well-lit selfie... no duck faces please!), and choose a font that matches your style. You might include some punchy hot pinks or oranges if you are an energetic powerhouse, or maybe some subdued blues and greens for those with a calmer vibe.

Keep your industry in mind too- something loud and creative like the Marketing field allows for more cheerful pops of color while something in Finance or Biotech may be a little more traditional and conservative. Either way, it is probably time to give your resume a facelift. Gone are the days of the lifeless resume that looks like an old newspaper! Spice it up like your favorite Spice Girl would (mine was Posh Spice... and you?).

Speaking of Spice Girls. Ever been to London? Those Brits love giant yellow 'Mind the Gap' signs on the subway. Not only for smoky underground railways full of Brits, but this also applies to your resume too! If you've been out of work (or never even had a "real job" for that matter) then it's time to fill in the blanks with transferable skills.

At some point in your life, I bet you have learned excellent skills for project management (navigating Whole Foods while sticking to a recipe card can count), conflict resolution (that one time you threw an acai bowl at your ex because he spoke before you had your third coffee), and leadership development (if you've ever been the Designated Driver, then you know what I mean), just to name a few. Don't be afraid to update your employment gaps and get creative. If you owned your own business, then you have pretty much worn every hat there is. Highlighting versatility and strong skill sets is sure to impress hiring managers.

And while you are at it, get over your past job titles! I see it so many times, boring resumes with boring titles from boring jobs with very technical names like Data Analyst II or Lead Client Services Consultant or Account Representative III. What do those even mean?! If you are in Marketing and want to transfer to a Sales role, then highlight all of your sales experience on your current resume, including your titles. If you had super technical jobs from big companies, then change your title to what you *actually* did.

"Know, first, who you are, and then adorn yourself accordingly."
-Epictetus

Make it easy for hiring managers and recruiters so they don't have to read between the lines (literally). Believe me, no one is calling your past company to have them pull your personnel record and list your exact job title in all of its technical glory. Data Analyst could get changed to Brand Analytics Coordinator if that is what it actually was, or Lead Client Services Consultant could get changed to Temp Talent Placement Specialist if that's what you were doing, or Account Representative III could be changed to Senior Sales Department Head if that's your jam. See? Cut the lame titles and highlight those that are going to help you land your next role in your fave industry.

When submitting your resume via automated Applicant Tracking Systems (ATS), be careful of your data not going into a black hole! Avoid keywords and parsing messiness and ensure your ATS uploads are strategic, clean, and hit the keywords listed in the job ad so that the application will not be rejected immediately. Even better, find the hiring manager and potential future teammates on LinkedIn. Connect with them to start a personal message thread and strike up a conversation!

Speaking of LinkedIn, expand your use of job search platforms like Monster, Indeed,

Glass Door, or CareerBuilder. I like LinkedIn the best! But be careful with the Easy Apply feature. Get targeted in your search and your applications. Don't blanket the earth with your resume! Steer clear of applying to a company's Social Media Manager role, Marketing Supervisor role, Graphic Designer role, and Ads Coordinator role all at the same time. Pick only your *best* fit! The one where you *know* you will be a shoo-in.

To cover letter or not to cover letter? That is the question.

The new modern cover letter is the message you send to the hiring manager on LinkedIn or the email you send where you attach your resume. I honestly do not recommend trying to apply on company websites because the algorithm and parsing can get messy. It is impersonal and you will most likely fall into a black hole where no one will even see your amazing self. By any possible means, find the hiring manager's name and email address, or even just try to connect with someone else in the company that could refer you directly to the role. That is what I mean by "cover letter." Personalizing always, there is no room for copy-pasting and generic crap here!

Find a way to tie in the company's mission vision values to your own, which implies that you have thoroughly reviewed their website. Why do you specifically align with the company? What value would you provide them by working on their team?

It seems our culture has evolved into the "What's in it for me?" train of thought and we forget that we are selling ourselves! It is super important to make ourselves sound as desirable as possible when "pitching" our services and skill sets to hiring managers. There isn't a magical fairy that's going to put pixie dust on our resumes that are lost in a Human Resources Information System (HRIS) and send it directly in front of the eyes of the hiring manager! Sorry, Charlie, you are going to have to work for it.

This ain't your mama's interview.

If you make it past the black hole applicant tracking system, the initial email coordination, and the phone screen, then you are on your way for that coveted in-person interview! Are you ready for some Interviewing 101 Cliff Notes, rapid-fire style?

Basics that I am sure you have heard before: arrive on time (or ten minutes early but any earlier is rude), smile, give a firm handshake, look your interviewer in the eye, and don't chew gum. Alright, but let's teach an old interviewing dog some new tricks!

Even though we live in the digital age, many hiring managers still appreciate a printout of your resume to look over when they are meeting with you. Print extra copies including one to have in front of you as well (just in case you forget who it was you worked for twelve years ago). Don't have a printer? No problem. There are several chains around the United States where you can pay as little as ten cents per page to print copies of your resume on standard 8x11 paper (oh and leave the bad 90s papyrus style "fancy resume" paper in the 90s please). Check out Postal Annex, UPS Store, FedEx Kinkos, Office Depot, or Staples for that printing fix. Place your resume copies in a simple manila folder or discreet document sleeve to keep from getting crumpled, or worse, folded up in your bag hot dog or hamburger style.

Bring a pen in case you have some forms to fill out and bring personally branded

business cards if you kept them from your previous adventures in networking.
When in doubt, overdress! Some companies are suit & tie, professional style, and some are much more casual, but either way, make sure you look sharp. If you are attending a virtual interview via video call, PJ pants are allowed just make sure you look great from the waist up! Wear a pop of color that is memorable- I love a good cerulean blue, fuchsia, or goldenrod yellow to help me stand out from the sea of all-black wearing interview bots. Red is typically a power color, blue a little more soothing, and green for money. Remember that crazy cat-lady art teacher you had as a sophomore in high school? She was definitely onto something when teaching you about color theory!

Always answer the tried and true "What are some of your weaknesses?" question with a positive answer.

For example, "I am a perfectionist, so I like to make sure all details are in order and everything is organized before hitting Send or completing a project." Or, "Since I am such a people lover, I tend to make friends very easily at work and want to spend tons of time in the office, but I think I need to set better boundaries with my work-life balance." These are perceived weaknesses that can be valuable to a hiring manager! Learn how to answer those tough "trick questions" and talk yourself up with ease.

What to do afterward? Always send a quick thank-you, whether that is via email, LinkedIn message, or handwritten note. Typically, a digital thanks can be done after a phone interview but after a long process of multiple interviewers or an in-person interview, a snail-mail thank you note is an old-school way of showing that you give a sht about the job. This was a super common practice back in the early 2000s, but somewhere along the way we all got too sucked into our phones and Gmail accounts to add that personalized touch. Be the star student and stand out amongst the sea of applicants!

Not following up with your interviewers is like filling a bath without a drain stopper.

Be sure to follow up — don't let a hiring manager or recruiter "ghost" you like those dudes on Tinder. Make sure you wait a week or so after your thank-you is sent, then feel free to send a quick email just to check-in. Giving it a week shows that you are eager, but not too eager and that you are interested but also patient with their process. Don't let all your hard work go down the drain!

When asked to provide references, be wary of using your boyfriend or best friend just because the hiring manager "will never find out." Don't start your new job process off on the lying foot! Tap into your LinkedIn network to catch up with former colleagues, supervisors, and managers and grab their contact info, *only after asking* if they would be able to take a few minutes to provide a reference. You can also use previous customers, clients, or business partners to help you seal the deal.

Pivoting with Purpose Tip

Get your resume into tip-top shape, personalize that cover letter, and nail those interviews. It's your time to shine.

Chapter 13:

Let's Talk About Money, Honey

Everybody's *not-so-favorite* subject. For whatever reason in our American culture, money is always one of those taboo or uncomfortable topics for people. If you have not worked on your money mindset, then you might not be in a place to understand how the energy of it works.

My dad grew up in Turkey, a developing country, where he was taught to save everything. We're talking sardine cans, butter tins, plastic yogurt containers, newspapers, allll the things! Fast forward to his adult life and moving to America where there were shiny new things to hoard like junk mail, plastic grocery bags, real estate agent magnets, logo pens from plumbers & carpet cleaners & window washers & every other company within a 5-mile radius — you name it, he saved it.

The fact that I grew up in a hoarding household is one of the main reasons that I am a minimalist today! It's also why I launched my residential decluttering business — to help others like my dad. Over the years in my business, Let's Get you Organized, I helped *hundreds* of homeowners in transforming their fixed mindset that there will never be enough, they will never have enough, and that they have to save every little thing to feel safe and secure.

Take a pulse on your money mindset. What beliefs about money do you currently hold? Where did those beliefs come from? My dad not only collected what would be considered most people's trash, but he also hoarded money too. My entire childhood was all about "saving for a rainy day" and never letting ourselves experience joy financially. I'm sure you've heard the saying "Money doesn't grow on trees." Chances are, all the beliefs you currently have about money were passed on to you from your parents. Think of it as your guilt inheritance. A lovely little gift of weird yucky feelings about cash, a lifetime of restriction (or overspending and overshopping on the other end of the spectrum).

What stories have been passed down to you? Take time to reflect on this as later in this chapter we will dive into the whole reason you're probably looking for a job in the first place... your paycheck! Having a healthy money mindset is *crucial* when negotiating future salaries and wages. Don't skimp on this part!

"Money is only a tool. It will take you wherever you wish, but it will not replace you as the driver."
-Ayn Rand

I grew up in an environment where I was only allowed to have one pair of shoes per school year, my family could only eat out on Friday nights (with the choice between three reasonably priced restaurants), and we could only take one vacation per year (always to our family home in Turkey where room, board, and entertainment were already free... not to mention the crazy low exchange rate). As a first-generation American, I do appreciate my dad's thrift and ability to reuse, reduce, and recycle.... But as a kid in the 90s, it was tough not to have the hot pink glitter jelly sandals, the Lunchables & Gushers & Fruit by the Foots in my lunchbox, and the Disney character backpacks. Being frivolous with money was for *other* people, after all.

I was lucky enough to be making six figures at the age of 28, but I never spent any of that money. I left the twat boss job with over *$30,000* in savings. Is that normal for a 28-year-old? It was normal for someone that was taught to save and scrunch every last penny, you bet! It took *years* for me to rewrite my money story, but it was the ACTION that made all the difference.

See, I invested in my very first business coach in 2018. And she cost more than my car. After hitting "send" on that giant amount, magic started to happen. I realized that money is just energy, that there was more where that came from, and that by hiring her I'd created a container for myself to expand. I had skin in the game. I had finally invested in myself and the belief that I knew I could start my own business and leave my corporate job behind.

Everything started to change in my life once I started to fix my relationship with money. Instead of dreading spending money, I joyfully took friends out to dinner, bought the "fancy" wine, added guac every time I ate at my fave burrito joint, and upgraded my tiny sedan to a luxury SUV. I never went into debt, all hell did not break loose, the sky didn't fall, and I was not suddenly considered a bad person for having a new love affair with cash. It was terrifying to drop a ton of cash at once (on something that wasn't even tangible, like coaching) but it was exactly what I needed to do to erase all of those unhealthy money mindset issues that I had since childhood!

Know your worth... and then add tax.

If you've made it to the Offer Letter stage, then huge congrats are in order! Most companies will give you a formal written agreement in PDF format or an online portal with electronic signature capability. Always be sure to get an offer in writing that includes the full job description and payment information. Until it's signed by all parties, don't leave your current job or start telling all of your friends and making a big announcement to your network! Wait until the (digital) ink dries.

We know that money is an *amazing* thing and for many, that's the whole point of working, right? Hop online to ensure that the rate offered is on point with what people in your area at the same level of experience are making. There are several free salary tools on the web to help you benchmark pay rates. Find the new job title, location, and industry that most closely relates to the job you're being offered and go from there. This is called "compensation analysis" in the world of (boring) HR. "Comp" changes amid *tons* of factors including geographic location, field, industry, size of the company, years of experience, and more.

If you are an Executive Assistant living in Houston, working for a large corporation, then you're not going to have the same pay range as your Executive Assistant friend in Nebraska with the same type of role that works for a small mom & pop business. If you are a Business Development Manager in the trucking industry in Arkansas, your pay is probably not the same as a Business Development Manager in the hospitality industry in Connecticut. See what I mean?

Many job seekers don't realize that these tools are readily available and can be super helpful when trying to decide on how to negotiate your next salary!

Get clear on the company's total compensation and rewards as well. If your past role offered full medical, dental, and vision benefits plus a 401(k)-company match, tuition reimbursement, and a flexible spending account, then make sure you know the cost of those if you're accepting an offer at a new role without all the perks!

Are you surviving or are you thriving?
There are varying beliefs on negotiating salaries but I for one believe that you should negotiate because you're essentially locking yourself into a contract with that company and agreeing to that pay rate for the unforeseen future. You never know if the economy will take a hit, if the company will have issues, or if raises will suddenly no longer be available.

"Money will only make you more of what you already are."
-T Harv Eker

How can you decide what you'll accept and what you'll negotiate? Create a Survive vs Thrive budget. Grab your pen & paper or digital note-taking tool and write out how much you would need just to survive (rent or mortgage, car payment & insurance, gas, groceries, toiletries, utilities, student loans, whatever your true obligations are). Then think of the things that are "nice to haves" like a gym membership, nail appointments, a dog walker, organic foods, retirement fund contributions, and whatever else your heart desires. From there you can reverse engineer the numbers so that you have a game plan when negotiating your rate.

Pivoting with Purpose Tip

Do your homework, know what you're worth, and discover what you need to not only survive, but thrive. Stop being scared of money and stop shying away from talking about it. It is time to step up to the plate and start asking for what you are worth! Set the standard for what that number is and then go out there and get it.

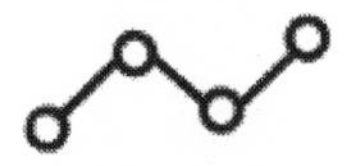

Chapter 14:

EQ Is the New IQ

A company is more likely to hire you based on your emotional intelligence than on your big brain intelligence. In the new, modern, culture-centric era of Human Resources and Talent Acquisition, the old days of "personnel" departments are gone. Lately, generic job titles like Director of HR or Personnel Manager are much less common than the Director of People & Talent or Employee Wellness Manager. This is the new world of work! People tend to get trapped into thinking that HR departments are only there to make sure our payroll goes through, our benefits get deducted accurately, and we are getting our annual performance reviews plus salary increases. These days, HR departments are here to ensure that their company is moving towards building a healthy culture with engaged & fulfilled employees that are role-aligned in their job duties and value-aligned with the company's core mission.

Candidates that can work in large, collaborative, cross-functional teams, are much more desirable than individual contributors that prefer to work in silos. When writing your resume, your cover letter, your LinkedIn bio, and your follow-ups to posted openings be sure to highlight that you not only know what emotional intelligence is but that you actively work to ensure you are developing it!

You know that adage, "Choose your boss, not your job." That rings true here too. If you don't love (or even like) the people you work with day in and day out, then how can you enjoy your life? You can't. But you *can* change your perspective and up your emotional intelligence game.

It starts with understanding your strengths, as well as others'. Honoring those different skill sets, personality types, and communication styles can go a long way in bringing in more diverse perspectives and experiences in your life. But at first, that can feel uncomfortable af.

I urge you to *get curious.*

Curious about why your boyfriend acts the way he does when you ask him to put his dishes in the dishwasher. Curious about why you won't simply go downstairs to your lower level apartment neighbor to request that she turns her music down when it is legitimately shaking your entire upstairs unit (not to mention shaking your level of sanity). Curious about why your friend has completely ghosted you but you continue to tell yourself you "have no idea why" even though that shtty thing you said to her a few weeks ago is haunting you, deep down.

Get curious. Become a more emotionally intelligent human being and begin to understand others' viewpoints and perspectives — it can make you more likable and also make you like others more! Win-win.

Remember those personality tests I mentioned in a previous chapter? Those come into play here! Knowing yourself, your triggers, your pet-peeves, and your personal work to do is *super* important as you develop your EQ!

As you are on the journey to aligning your *tactical* skill sets to your next role in life, don't forget to honor those *emotional* skill sets as well.

"75 percent of careers are derailed for reasons related to emotional competencies, including inability to handle interpersonal problems during times of difficulty or conflict; or inability to adapt to change or elicit trust."

-Center for Creative Leadership

Having a high EQ is an amazing trait, but we all have our work to do. Personal development is an ongoing journey and there is never an endpoint! In any workplace, there are always going to be triggers that bring out your ego. Coworkers, bosses, clients, vendors, teammates, project managers, and all of the other people that you interact with can be like little landmines in your career progression. Make sure that if you accidentally step on one, you get curious and start to do the inner work in questioning your ego. We all want to take pride in our work and be recognized for our achievements, but let's be real: humans are complex beings and are sometimes pretty damn difficult to work with!

Relationship building and communication are key in the workplace. Nobody wants to go to a job where they don't get along with their team, so it's up to you to become the person that attracts friends and healthy relationships in the workplace. Karens are going to Karen and there's always going to be situations where you need to "be the bigger person."

Remember that old story about the tortoise and the hare? If you're not a huge fan of water cooler conversations, dislike dilly-dallying, and can't wait to get out of conversations with slow talkers — take a step back. Put yourself in the other person's shoes and begin to honor others' strengths and personality traits. We can all accomplish the same goals with different routes and plans to get there. Don't burn a bridge at your job because you're more like a hare than a tortoise. Different personalities in the office can support each other like yin & yang — stay away from being combative at work! Display your emotional intelligence by collaborating together as a team and solve your interpersonal issues.

Level up.

Think of EQ as a video game. You're always trying to get to the next level. Beating the "big boss" at the end of each level, means overcoming triggering situations at work.

Mustered up the courage to speak with your passive-aggressive coworker that keeps moving your lunch in the fridge? Setting boundaries like a boss — **level up!**

Simmered on an email and waiting to respond until you were no longer in an emotionally agitated state? Practicing self-awareness like a pro — **level up!**

Or maybe you failed to speak up about a project you wanted before a coworker snatched it up. After the meeting, you then reflected on what went wrong, vowing to yourself that you will speak up during project planning sessions, and stay engaged and present in each meeting so that you're not distracted or multitasking on other things and miss the opportunity to opt-in next time — **level up!**

"Let's not forget that the little emotions are the great captains of our lives and we obey them without realizing it."

-Vincent van Gogh

This isn't just homework for the sake of homework — homing in on your EQ level can help in all areas of your life. Chances are, if you bottle up small triggers in the workplace then you also bottle up on the same issues when interacting with your family, your spouse, or your friends. The beauty of working in and on your EQ is that it affects not only your professional life but also your personal life. Your work relationships mirror your personal relationships.

Assess where you are and where you want to be so that you can easily identify the gap. Read personal development books, go to seminars, attend training sessions, watch YouTube videos, listen to podcasts, meditate — it's time to practice mindfulness. Working on your EQ is a lifetime of work and it is definitely a journey but as soon as you are aware of your current behavioral traits, you can change the areas that aren't serving you.

Self-reflection and mindfulness are always going to help you beat that big bad boss at the end of every level. It's an exciting game to play! Imagine the personal rewards and feelings of achievement and accomplishment that can come with developing this skill.

Many times, I see job jumpers that are hopping from one role to the next, not for career progression or a higher salary, but simply because they can't solve their issues with the people around them. If you're having issues at one organization and fail to level up your EQ, those same issues are going to follow you to the next company. People issues are people issues and they don't just disappear! It starts with you. And it starts with EQ.

Pivoting with Purpose Tip

Don't lose your coveted, fresh new job, over one triggering coworker or boss. Learn how to stop being an a**hole- your future boss and coworkers will thank you for it. Level up your emotional intelligence game and solve your problems like a big girl (or boy).

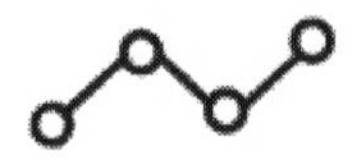

Chapter 15:

This Isn't the End

This is the beginning of your journey to pivoting with purpose! No more living a life that's "just" anything. Stop being a "Just Girl" or a "Just Guy." You know, like *"It's just a job"* or *"It's just a steppingstone"* or *"It's just temporary"* or *"It's just my intense feelings of impending doom because I'm not fulfilling my true life's purpose."*

I never want anyone to rot alone in a cubicle or settle for a life that's "good enough." I don't want people to live their life based on what society, or their parents, or their spouse, or their friends think they should be doing. I don't want people to die with dreams in their hearts and bucket lists unchecked. That's why I wrote this book — to teach others to navigate the journey of purpose finding and souls calling so they can up-level their lives. I'm focused on making sht happen and helping my clients do the same. Taking action is the name of my game. My specialty is in helping busy, overworked, underpaid, unfulfilled people that are ready to take action and change their lives for the better — whether that's by getting organized, changing their mindset, or opting in to following their purpose and utilizing their natural skills, talents, and gifts.

Hopefully, by now, you understand the mindset work that needs to be done to embrace your purpose, discover personal values, and release the limiting beliefs & anchors holding you back from opting into the life you deserve. Hopefully, by now, you understand that you were born with natural gifts, talents, skills, and abilities. Hopefully, by now, you realize that it's not up to other people to determine the direction of your life.

I constantly get asked how I got a job after burning out as an entrepreneur. I thought I was a "sellout" for leaving my business behind. But instead of my network judging or shaming me for getting a J.O.B., several people came out of the woodwork to ask me how I re-entered the workforce after being out of the 9-5 world for several years!

How did my skills translate? How did I use my network and connections to land the perfect role? Did it take me 500 applications, 25 interviews, and 2 offers to finally find my dream role? Yes, yes it did. And now I coach others on how to do the same. It does work, but it IS a numbers game. The competition is out there, and it's not fluffy work to be done.

There's no-BS here. Are you ready to move differently so you can have excitingly thrilling, amazingly positive, and utterly extraordinary outcomes?

I see so many people just toiling away with dreams in their hearts and items on their bucket list that will probably never get checked off. Clocking in and out mindlessly, like everyone else in the rat race. STOP IT NOW. You don't have to stick with the status quo by going on the route of grade school to college to 9-5 job to living paycheck to paycheck for the rest of your life, stuck in the hamster wheel and the rat race. There is more out there! It's about doing the work to figure out that sweet spot of doing the work you LOVE and blending that with what you can get PAID to do! Pivot with purpose. It's time.

ABOUT THE AUTHOR

Melisa lives in San Diego, California, and is the CEO of Make SHT Happen LLC. A direct & efficient professional, Melisa has over 10 years' experience in transforming processes that build successful companies! Melisa streamlines systems & creates simplified solutions for small business owners. She is a master of productivity, time management, and process improvement. She has a knack for digging deep with C-Level execs to achieve goals strategically and discover uniquely differentiating needle movers that increase profitability. Melisa spoke on over fifteen stages in 2019 with her keynote topics that garnered attention from over 50 national news publications as well as 5,000 clients, customers, and loyal fans! Her signature talks are on productivity. They include life-changing tips on time management, decluttering, minimalism, organization, and goal setting. An inspiring & motivating speaker, Melisa's energy is sure to light up any crowd! Melisa also finds joy in helping perfectionistic millennials & burnt out entrepreneurs clarify their PURPOSE to bridge the gap between current circumstances and their future. At her company, Let's Get You Hired, she gives her clients the customized roadmap they need to succeed with powerful values exercises to determine the best culture fit, tools to clean up a digital footprint, plus storytelling and copywriting activities to boost confidence and credibility. Her programs will help you learn why your resume is not getting you to the top of the pile, why LinkedIn should be your best friend, how to answer those tough interview questions, and how to implement impactful follow-up tactics.

Check out www.makeshthappen.biz to learn more about current programs and join Melisa's email list to keep your momentum going!

Made in the USA
Columbia, SC
12 October 2020